Homes

Salvador Sarmiento

Illustrated with photos

HAMPTON-BROWN BOOKS
MANY CULTURES, MANY LANGUAGES...MANY POSSIBILITIES!™

There are homes
in the country,

and homes in the city.

There are homes
in the mountains,

and homes by the sea.

There are homes
in the desert,

and homes on the water.

7

There are homes on the
street where I live!